KING EDMUND, SAINT AND MARTYR

a casket of wonders

Words by Tim Holt Wilson
Paintings by Brian Whelan

Roseberry
Crest

INTRODUCTION

The story of King Edmund of East Anglia, Christian saint and martyr, is truly a casket of wonders. His richly-decorated tomb in Bury St Edmunds Abbey was a centre for pilgrimage in the Middle Ages, and has continued to feed our imagination 460 years after its destruction, thanks to eye-witness accounts of its glory days. Since Abbo of Fleury first put pen to parchment in 985 a succession of monks, poets, scholars and religious devotees have written much about St Edmund, some searching for facts, others embroidering fantasies in their quest for a good story.

Can anything new grow in this over-worked ground? This short book endeavours to trace a 'thin red line' through the *mythos* of St Edmund, where the body of fiction has been discreetly joined to the severed head of truth. It will attempt to do justice to the intricacy of this historical and religious heritage, which is an integral part of the popular mythology of East Anglia and which even now excites controversy.

The striking artwork of Brian Whelan which adorns this book is ideal for visually representing this wealth. Like a miraculous wolf holding a shouting head between his paws, Whelan is a new, imaginative guardian of Edmund's fascinating legacy of fact and fable.

1. KING EDMUND'S WORLD

Edmund ruled the kingdom of East Anglia between 855 and 869, and was its last independent king. What little we know about his reign is drawn from a handful of historical sources, including coinage.

The name Edmund means 'Prosperity Protector' in Old English. The people of East Anglia were predominantly English speakers at this time, although some may still have spoken the Welsh Celtic language of their Romano-British ancestors[1]. The new science of population genetics suggests that while there had been some immigration of Germanic and Scandinavian people into East Anglia in the 5th and 6th centuries, about three-quarters of the population were descended from island British stock[2]. It is likely that Edmund's ancestors were members of an immigrant minority whose Germanic language and culture came to dominate their new homeland.

Edmund's social world was very different from our own. At this time society was broadly organised into four classes of people: firstly, the warriors, a group which included the king and his nobles, the earls, ealdormen and thanes; secondly, those who prayed, including priests, monks and nuns; thirdly, the freeman commoners or churls, including farmers and peasants and also craft workers and specialist servants; fourthly the slaves. The last two classes made up the bulk of the population by whose toil and products the lives of the other two classes were maintained and enhanced.

For all classes, there were two important social ties: kinship, in which relationships between men were paramount and a woman's role and position depended on that of her husband, and service to a lord. In Edmund's case, as we shall see, it is possible that, as a devout Christian as well as a king, he considered himself bound to no overlord other than God.

The Land of the East Angles

The geography of Edmund's kingdom was different from that of today. Sea levels were slightly higher, which meant that broad estuaries teeming with fish and wildfowl extended far inland in many eastern coastal areas, and also south of the Wash in what is now Marshland. The Fens were a wilderness of meres and reed beds dotted with occasional islands, where big, sluggish rivers such as the Nene and Ouse drained to the sea.

By this time most parts of the Norfolk and Suffolk claylands and sandlands had been settled, and the ancestors of today's villages had been founded, with familiar English names such as those ending in *–ton*, *–ham* or *–ingham*, though not necessarily on the same sites as today.

These settlements, known as 'vills', were socially and economically a part of estates owned by the king and his nobility or controlled by the church. They were associations of farmsteads engaged in subsistence agriculture and also supplying food and other products for their lord's *halh* (hall).

King Edmund's royal estates in Suffolk would have included Bures, Exning, Blythburgh and probably Kingshall at Bradfield St George. The landscape associated with these 'vills' would have looked well ordered, with fields, lanes, hedges, ditches, woods and coppices. By contrast, many valleys were a swampy wilderness, and tracts of wildwood are likely to have remained, particularly in high clayland areas, as implied by *ley* and *field* names which may be linked with clearings in woodland.

We also have evidence for Danish settlement, probably in the decades after 870, in the form of Scandinavian place names containing *–by*, *thorp*, and *toft*. The only place in East Anglia that could be described as a town was *Gippeswic* (Ipswich), which was an important centre for overseas trade, particularly with the Rhineland, and produced a distinctive type of pottery known as Ipswich Ware. It may have had a population of more than 2000[3].

Monastic centres in King Edmund's time included Brandon, Burgh Castle, North Elmham and West

into East Anglia from the west, the Icknield Way corridor[4].

The mapped distribution of Ipswich Ware pottery gives a rough indication of the likely extent of Edmund's kingdom. It included the counties of Norfolk and Suffolk, bounded to the north and east by the sea. Its southern boundary was the River Stour; its south-western boundary lay along the Devil's Dyke near Newmarket. The Fens formed its western boundary, running from Ely northwards to Wisbech and the River Nene.

A Boy King

There are two main sources of information about King Edmund's origins. The earliest is 'The Passion of St Edmund' by Abbo of Fleury, which says that Edmund was born of kingly forefathers and was descended from a noble Old Saxon lineage, *ex Antiquorum Saxonum nobili prosapia oriundus*[5]. The second source is Geoffrey of Wells, a later writer who believed that Abbo was referring to continental Saxony[6]. He relates a story that Edmund was adopted by a childless king of East Anglia named Offa, who had met Edmund while he was passing through Germany on his way to Jerusalem to pray for an heir. This story is attractive but not historically reliable. There is no corroborating historical evidence of a 9th century king of East Anglia called Offa. Indeed one of Geoffrey's

Dereham, and there were many island sites in the Fens: 'these marshes provide many communities of monks with a welcome haven of solitary society', as Abbo of Fleury put it, including Ely, Soham and Ramsey. A major earthwork, the Devil's Dyke, defended the most important overland access route contemporaries, John of Wallingford, refutes this fable of Edmund's continental origins, saying that 'certain writers' have twisted the story of St Botolph to fit that of St Edmund[7]. However the fabulation continued: a late 14th century source names Edmund's parents as Alkmund and Siwara from Nuremberg in Germany[8].

It seems most likely that Edmund was a member of the old East Anglian royal family or at least one of the old nobility. In an earlier paragraph of his book, Abbo places the Saxons among the 'three peoples of Germany' who had expelled the Britons and divided up the country for themselves. He says that East Anglia 'fell by lot' to the Saxons, which suggests we need not read any continental meanings into his use of the term 'Saxon'.

Continuing his fable of Edmund's continental origins, Geoffrey relates that he first landed on the Norfolk coast, at a place called *Maidenebure* ('Maidenbower') near Hunstanton. He came to a river where he knelt to pray. As he got up *duodecim limpidissimi fontes de terra eruperunt,* 'twelve of the clearest springs burst forth from the ground'. Continuing his journey, Edmund eventually arrived at Attleborough, where he was delayed for a year by 'the Devil', but spent his time profitably learning the Psalter by heart.

The Chronicle of the Priory of St Neot may be a more reliable source of information about Edmund's accession to power. It states that Edmund ascended the throne of East Anglia on Christmas Day in 855 at the age of 14. He was consecrated 'with great rejoicing' the following year by Hunbercht, Bishop of the East Angles, at the *villa regia* (royal 'vill') at *Burna* in Suffolk. Traditionally, *Burna* has been identified as Bures in south Suffolk, although rival locations at Maidenhall and Sudbourne have been suggested.

Abbo says that Edmund was a professing Christian from his early years, and compelled to rule by popular choice. He is described as attractive and graced with eloquence and humility, and as dwelling as lord among his contemporaries *mirabilis mansuetudine*, 'with extraordinary kindness'.

Edmund came to the throne in turbulent times. Within ten years he would be forced to fight against Danish invaders for the survival of his kingdom.

2. THE INVASION

The first Viking raid on England took place in the year 787, says the Anglo-Saxon Chronicle[9]. In 793 the famous monastery at Lindisfarne was destroyed and the monks slaughtered. For over two centuries the long-ships came and went around the coast of Britain and Ireland, killing and plundering as they pleased, raiding inland under their Raven banner then returning home to Scandinavia with booty each autumn. This prolonged plague of violence has its source in Scandinavian society, which was driven by competition for wealth and honour among its warrior class, with shortage of land a contributory factor. The Viking war-bands came initially for plunder and later for land to settle.

In 865 the heathen host swooped on the rich farmlands and monasteries of East Anglia: 'And in the same year a great heathen army came to England, and took winter-quarters from the East Anglians'. It is difficult to judge how many men constituted a 'great army' but about a thousand would be a realistic figure. We are told the East Anglians provided them with horses and sued for peace. The army spent the next three years ravaging Northumbria and Mercia, before returning to East Anglia in 869, where they took up winter quarters at Thetford. As the Anglo-Saxon Chronicle puts it: 'And the same year St Edmund the king fought with them, and the Danes took victory, and slew the king and overran all the country and destroyed all the monasteries they came to'. A late version of the Chronicle adds that 'the names of the leaders who slew the king were Ingware and Ubba'.

Who were Inguar and Ubba?

The earliest link between Inguar and Ubba and King Edmund is found in Abbo. Abbo characterises them as Danish emissaries of the devil who came to Edmund to test his faith *indurati frigore suae malitiae*, 'hardened by the coldness of their malice'. They originate among the savage peoples of the North, he says, followers of Antichrist who carry the mark of the Beast on their foreheads.

Later writers embroidered lively stories about Inguar and Ubba. The earliest is Roger of Hoveden, who named them as sons of Lothbroc. The Chronicles of Hyde Abbey relate that Hyngwar died while trying to cross a ford at Hungerford, while Hubba was swallowed alive by the earth while out riding. Geoffrey of Wells relates that Ubba was a practicer of *maleficia*, 'the black arts', and would ask to be raised up before a battle so he

could cast an evil eye over the opposing forces to guarantee victory[10].

Roger of Wendover preserves a story which provides a motive for their invasion of East Anglia[11]. He says that a member of the Danish royal family named  Lothbroc was blown out to sea in a boat and eventually was washed up at *Redham* in Norfolk. He was taken before King Edmund and received with honour at his court. One day Lothbroc was jealously killed by the king's huntsman named Bern.

When the crime came to light, Bern was punished by being set adrift in Lothbroc's old boat. By chance he was blown to Denmark. People recognised the boat, and took him before Hinguar and Hubba who demanded to know what had become of their father. Bern made up a story that Lothbroc had been killed at Edmund's command. Hinguar and Hubba swore to the gods to avenge their father's death, and set sail for East Anglia with an army of 20,000 soldiers.

A more lurid story is recounted by Thomas of Elmham. Inguar and Ubba were said to be the sons of a bear sired on the daughter of the King of Denmark. One day Edmund was passing through Denmark and was shocked to catch the bear *in flagrante delicto* with a woman, and promptly cut off his head. Thus the sons invaded East Anglia and killed Edmund to avenge their father's death[12].

The Scandinavian sources provide more information about Inguar and Ubba. They are said to be two of the sons of Ragnar Lothbroc, who was the most famous Viking of the ninth century. Saxo[13] states that he had seven children, among them Ivar and Ubbi. In the Icelandic *Ragnars Saga*, Inguar is named Ivar the Boneless.

By the time Abbo was writing in the 980s it seems likely the names of Inguar and Ubba had become attached to the narrative of Edmund's martyrdom, if only for the sake of a good story. They provided a suitably satanic counterpart to Edmund's Christian virtues.

3. MARTYRDOM

Abbo is the creative intelligence behind the cult of St Edmund. He was one of the leading scholars of his time in France, and was familiar with the value of miracles as evidence for sainthood, and of martyrdom for fostering faith in difficult times. While Abbo describes Edmund's death in elaborate detail, other contemporary sources merely state that he was killed by the Danes.

Abbo was staying at the new monastery at Ramsey between 986 and 987. He describes the circumstances surrounding the origins of his book in its preface. He was asked by the monks to write down the story of the *mirabilium patratoris Eadmundi regis et martyris passionem*, 'the Passion of Edmund the worker of miracles, king and martyr'. Accounts of the lives and deaths of saints and martyrs were popular instructional reading in the early Church, and a staple item of fare at monastic establishments. The Edmund story, we are told, had never been written down before, but had been told to the monks by Archbishop Dunstan, who in turn had heard it in his youth from an aged man who had once been Edmund's armour-bearer.

An English Saint Sebastian

As we have seen, the Anglo-Saxon Chronicle for 869 states that 'St Edmund the king fought with them, and the Danes took victory, and slew the king and overran all the country...' Abbo takes up the story when the battle is lost and the kingdom lies in ruins. Inguar interrogates some local people and finds out that the king is at a settlement called *Haegelisdun*. He sends a messenger to demand the king's surrender, while he follows behind with his army. The king confers with one of his bishops, who counsels him to submit to these demands and save himself by flight. Edmund says his conscience will not allow him to flee when so many of his subjects have lost their lives, and that he will voluntarily surrender himself. The only master he is willing to serve is Christ. He tells the messenger that the Christian king Edmund would rather die than submit to a pagan chief, unless he first converts to Christianity. Inguar arrives with his army. Edmund is bound like Christ before Pilate, mocked, beaten then tied to a tree and scourged, all the while calling on Christ. This infuriates his captors, who pierce him all over his body with the spikes of arrows as if engaged in target practice. He is so riddled with darts that he looks like a hedgehog or thistle, resembling St Sebastian in his Passion. He continues to call out to Christ so Inguar orders his body to be pulled off the bloody tree and his head to be cut off. The Danes take away the head then throw it into a thicket of thorns or brambles.

Abbo is at pains to emphasise the precedents for this kind of death, making parallels between the Passions of Christ and St Sebastian and that of Edmund, which give him a place among the illustrious company of martyrs. For example, he follows the 5th century *Acta S. Sebastiani Martyris* in describing the saint as looking like a hedgehog, and there are obvious parallels between the piercing of the body on the blood-stained tree and the Passions of Christ and Sebastian.

There are also precedents in Scandinavian sources for cruel and unusual deaths being meted out to a royal prisoner who refuses to submit. Saxo describes how Haldan of Denmark led a pirate expedition into Swedish territory. He killed the Swedish king then captured his nephew Erik, who *mori quam obsequi praeoptavit*, 'preferred to die rather than submit', for 'virtue does not know how to buy safety at the price of shame'. Erik is taken into the wilderness, shackled and left there to be eaten by wild animals. Similar treatment is given to the sons of King Volsung in the *Völsunga Saga*, and all but one are devoured by a she-wolf 'both great and evil of aspect'[14].

In keeping with the religious theme of martyrdom, Abbo emphasises Edmund's willingness to surrender and to die if needs be. He could, of course, have chosen to submit to a Danish warlord and pay him homage and tribute, as some of his fellow English kings did. However, like Saxo's Erik, he refused to do so, presumably because he considered himself as a sovereign king who acknowledged no overlord except God. His refusal to pay homage sealed his death warrant and made him a martyr.

It is impossible to disentangle fact from fiction in the death of King Edmund. We only have the evidence of a single account at third hand, which the author claims is based on the testimony of someone (Dunstan) who knew somebody (the armour-bearer) who claimed to

have first-hand evidence about the death. We cannot even know whether Edmund intended to sacrifice his life. We must accept Abbo's account, with his story of a Christian king who decided to abandon his two greatest assets, his life and kingdom, for the sake of resisting oppression and asserting his religious identity.

4. A NEW SAINT

The cult of St Edmund begins with the story of the king's severed head. Abbo says the armour-bearer saw it taken away by the Danes into *Haegelisdun* wood, but he did not know what had been done with it. Local people were able to recover the headless body then set about finding the head. As they searched through the wood the severed head 'broke into voice without help from [vocal] chords or service from the windpipe in the chest', and shouted to them 'Here! Here! Here!'. Then, says Abbo, God added another

miracle by providing the head with an unexpected guardian in the form of an enormous wolf which held it between its paws. The wolf is said to have tamely followed the people out of the wood to the place of burial, before returning to its former haunts, and 'never again did a wolf of such terrible aspect appear in that locality'.

This is a good story, and the image of the king's head between the paws of a wolf became one of the emblems of the saint. It is perhaps intended by Abbo to reinforce the Christian message about the power of God to transform the unredeemed beast in mankind.

Having been collected from the care of the wolf, Abbo says the head was reunited with the body, and both were buried nearby in a building of crude workmanship, in which they rested for many years. Archdeacon Hermann, writing in the late 11th century, describes this as 'a very small prayer-house' at a place called *Suthtune* (Sutton). The most likely location for this burial place is at Sutton Hall, a farmstead situated some 6 miles southwest of Bury St Edmunds. As Dr Stanley West has pointed out, this is a mile away from a site named Hellesden Ley, and there are three Mediaeval place names including the name Kingshall in the nearby village of Rougham[15].

We are told that Edmund's body remained here for many years until the persecution of the Danes lessened. William of Malmesbury tells us that a blind man entered the building one night and his eyes were filled with celestial light. Archdeacon Hermann relates that a bright light was seen where the candlestick stood near the corpse[16]. Within 30 years of Edmund's death coins were being minted by King Alfred of Wessex with the name of 'Sc [Sanctus] Edmund Rex' on the reverse. His career as a saint had begun.

In 915 the body of the newly sanctified Edmund was moved from its rustic resting place to a purpose-built church at the nearby monastic centre of *Beadericeswyrð*, later Bury St Edmunds. Abbo describes it as an enormous building made of wooden planks. He describes miracles as taking place at this church. The most significant of these, and a confirmation of the king's sanctity, is the incorrupt appearance of his body. It appears 'whole and very much as if alive', which he attributes to Edmund's state of virginity. Furthermore, 'a certain woman of blessed remembrance' named Oswen had made it her annual custom to open the coffin and clip the hair and nails of the corpse. She noticed that the body had healed itself by being reunited with its severed head, leaving only a very thin wrinkle like a red line round the neck.

In 990 a monk named Egelwin (Ailwin) from St Benet's monastery at Hulme in Norfolk was appointed guardian of the shrine. His work involved curating the body; according to Archdeacon Hermann he cleaned it and combed its hair, keeping any stray hairs in a special box. The tranquility of this relationship was soon disturbed by events in the wider world.

Between 994 and 1014 Svein Forkbeard Haraldsson, king of Denmark, led a succession of Viking armies

across southern England, burning cities and routing the English militias in a quest for plunder and revenge. In 1010 the host arrived in Suffolk, and Egelwin decided to remove the saint's shrine to safety.

He hired a cart and set out with it for London. A miracle is said to have taken place at the bridge over the River Lea at Stratford By Bow, where the cart was too wide for the bridge but managed to pass over it with one wheel suspended in mid-air.

The saint's body processed through the streets and nineteen miracles are said to have occurred between Aldgate and St Paul's. For the next three years the shrine was installed in St Gregory's church close to St Paul's, although the Bishop of London is said to have tried to divert the saint's remains to his own church, and the Archbishop of Canterbury[17] wanted to buy the fragment of the True Cross which hung around the saint's neck. Eventually Egelwin set out back to Bury by way of Stapleford Abbots and Greensted church in Essex[18]. This was the year in which Svein Forkbeard made himself the undisputed ruler of England.

A glowing warrior

Svein met his nemesis, we are told, one cold night in February 1014. He had recently imposed a heavy tax on his subjected realm. The people of Bury appealed to the supernatural power of St Edmund for help. The saint appeared in a dream to Egelwin telling him to take a personal message of protest to Svein, Egelwin set off for the Vikings' winter camp at Gainsborough and bravely delivered his message to the tyrant, who is said to have received it with fury. Lucky to escape with his life, Egelwin set off home.

A few days later he encountered some Danish horsemen on the road who told him their king was dead. They said Svein had been woken in the night by a vision of a glowing warrior with a spear, who struck him.

"Help, comrades, St. Edmund is killing me!" he shouted, before falling mortally wounded. Hermann claimed that he received this story from Egelwin himself. Other sources however just record that Svein died suddenly.

The death of Svein is probably the single most significant miraculous story claimed by the cult of St Edmund. Its power cannot be under-estimated. It claimed that the most terrifying Viking of the age, before whom all England was powerless, had been laid low by the saint.

The story was repeated down the centuries: the 13th century Icelandic author Snorri Sturluson mentions it in his Saga of St Olaf. The Svein story told by Egelwin laid the foundations for Edmund's status as England's patron saint and supernatural protector.

Svein's son Knut invaded England in 1015 and became king two years later. He was careful to treat St Edmund with great respect. In 1020 he approved the introduction of a community of Benedictine monks to maintain the shrine at Bury and granted special privileges to the new abbey[19] Beadericeswyrð became known as Sancte Eadmundes Byrig, St Edmund's Bury, and work began on building a new church. In 1032 a new, stone-built minster with a circular ground-plan was dedicated to St Mary and St Edmund.

The body and relics of St Edmund lay in a wooden reliquary or coffin in a curtained-off area next to the sanctuary.

We may gain an impression of the atmosphere of devotion surrounding this shrine from the miracle books compiled by Archdeacon Hermann and later Abbot Samson[20]. In 1044 King Edward the Confessor visited the Abbey and among his retinue was the Danish nobleman Osgod[21]. He is said to have proudly entered the shrine area wearing gold arm-rings and carrying a gilded axe over one shoulder, against the advice of bystanders. There he suddenly became mad and dashed himself against the walls of the building.

A few years later a dumb woman from Winchester called Aelfgeth was cured at the shrine. One night the saint came to her in a dream and complained that his coffin was becoming dusty and worm-eaten and that cobwebs were covering his face. Abbot Leofstan decided to open the coffin and check the condition of the body in the company of old Egelwin, now blind, and a chosen few. They lifted the body out onto a table and removed its coverings to reveal the serene face of the dead saint and the bloodstained shirt which he was wearing when he died. A powerful sweet odour filled the air. They removed the clothing to keep as separate relics, then wrapped the body in a linen sheet. Before replacing the body in its coffin, Leofstan decided to check whether the head really was joined onto the body. He arranged for a monk to hold the feet while he held the head; he tugged firmly at it, even pulling the monk towards him. Suddenly he became terrified and seems to have suffered a stroke: a paralysis seized him and his fingers became crippled.

This story suggests that the body may at some time have been prepared and embalmed. The use of aromatic preservatives such as myrrh and aloes for embalming is attested in the early Church, and Leofstan may have been able to tug at the head if it had been wired internally onto the body at some time. The thin red line around the neck noticed by Oswen in the early ninth century may be evidence of a discreet seam.

The shrine continued to enjoy royal patronage after the Norman Conquest. King William confirmed the privileges of the abbey, and supported Abbot Baldwin's ambitious plans to build a colossal church over the shrine[22]. Work had begun in the 880s, and had progressed sufficiently by 1095 for the relics of the saint to be installed in a new shrine, along with the relics of saints Botolph and Jurmin[23].

The change of regime was not without its problems however. The Abbey found that it needed to defend itself against the Norman bishop of East Anglia. In the 1060s Bishop Herfast proposed to move his seat from Thetford to St Edmund's Bury, which would have meant that Abbot Baldwin lost control of his abbey church. Baldwin immediately set out for Rome to ask the Pope to confirm the Abbey's privileges. This was granted, but the bishop would not take no for an answer and persisted in his claim. Shortly afterwards, Herfast was struck in the face by a branch while riding through a wood and blinded. Hermann says that his sight was only restored after he had been persuaded to prostrate himself on the steps of the altar at Bury, and had confessed his sin and begged God and St Edmund for forgiveness. Wisely the bishop decided to keep his seat in Thetford; it was later moved to Norwich by Bishop Herbert de Losinga[24], in about 1095.

Haegelisdun at Hoxne

This struggle between the bishop of East Anglia and the abbot had a long-lasting legacy, as it brought about the rise of Hoxne as a rival cult centre to Bury. Previous to this Hoxne had been a bishop's 'vill' with a church dedicated to another decapitated royal saint, Aethelbert of East Anglia[25].

In 1101 a charter of Herbert de Losinga mentions a chapel of St Edmund at Hoxne and claims it as the site of the saint's martyrdom. This chapel was part of Hoxne Priory, in turn part of Norwich Cathedral Priory, and it formed a nucleus around which a new cult of St Edmund could form in order to attract pilgrims and generate income. By the early 13th century Roger of Wendover was quoting *Hoxa* as the saint's first place of burial. By 1326 another chapel had been built in honour of the severed head[26].

Despite the long-standing claim of Hoxne to being the site of the martyrdom, scholars now agree that the name *Hoxa* cannot be derived from *Haegelisdun*. Hellesdon near Norwich or, as we have seen, Hellesden Ley at Bradfield St Clare have stronger claims on linguistic grounds[27].

Healing and Helping

While many vengeful stories are attributed to the powers of the Saint, the miracle books of Hermann and Samson record many more about his healing and helping powers, whether directly at the shrine or elsewhere. It is claimed that impediments of speech, sight and walking were miraculously cured, that people were saved from fever, theft, paralysis and drowning, and that the dead were restored to life.

At some time around 1050 a poor woman used to beg in the porch of the Abbey church. She had crippled legs and could only use her hands to get about with. She slept at night near the door. One night a pious Essex woman Aelfweve was keeping vigil at the shrine. She had a vision of a glowing figure who emerged from the area of the shrine. It glided down the nave of the darkened church towards the door,

made the sign of the cross over the sleeping beggar then returned whence it had come. The beggar woman woke up cured, jumped up and began crying out with joy, dancing and weeping.

We are also told that many miracles took place at sea. Invoking St Edmund was a considered efficacious against shipwreck, as in the case of a shipload of pilgrims returning from Rome in 1095 who were miraculously saved when they prayed to the saint after their vessel began to fill with water.

Saint Edmund also had power to confound thieves and help restore lost objects to their owners. Gerald of Wales describes a poor woman who used devoutly to kiss the offerings in front of St Edmund's shrine while at the same time sucking coins into her mouth. For this crime her lips became stuck to the altar[28].

5. AN ESTABLISHED SAINT

The venerable relics on display in the Abbey included an embroidered scarlet banner said to be the saint's standard in battle and which was reputed to have the power to extinguish fires. It showed the Tree of Knowledge with the serpent and Adam and Eve beneath a Lamb of God emblem in the centre of a gold circle against a background of stars[29]. This banner proved useful at the Battle of Fornham in 1173. While King Henry II was away fighting the Scots, his three sons and several powerful barons raised a rebellion. The Earl of Leicester landed in support of the rebel faction with a large army of Flemish mercenaries at Walton-on-the-Naze and then marched through Suffolk. The forces loyal to the king begged the abbot of Bury to lend them St Edmund's banner, and the two sides met in battle at Fornham St Genevieve near Bury. With the banner prominently visible, the king's forces were able to rout the rebel army, and returned victorious to the Abbey for a service of celebration.

Other relics on display included the saint's torn and blood-stained shirt which was kept in a glass case, his cup known as 'The Pardon Bowl' (it was reputed to have powers of healing and of pardoning sins), his sword, his psalter, the cart on which Egelwin carried his body to London, and the box of his hair and nail clippings collected by Oswen.

Shrine Design

In 1198 a serious accident befell the shrine. According to Jocelin of Brakelond[30] a candle fell during the night onto a draped wooden platform that stood nearby. Soon the area of the shrine was ablaze. Once the fire had been put out by the monks, they took stock of the damage. Much of the outside of the shrine had been ruined, but they were amazed to discover that the saint's coffin was undamaged and so was his cup, although the box in which it had been stored had been reduced to ashes. Luckily his shirt and other relics on display nearby had recently been temporarily removed due to renovation work.

Abbot Samson set about plans to redesign the shrine and check that the saint's body had not been affected.

The translation of the body from the old shrine to the new one took place on the Saint's day, November 20th. A few days later, Samson took a select group of twelve men with him and opened the coffin at dead of night. They found the corpse lying wrapped in silk and linen cloths, with its head joined to the body and raised on a small pillow. As he took the saint's head in his hands, Samson remembered stories about people who had been blighted for approaching the saint unworthily, and murmured prayers of entreaty. He then began to feel the saint's body: he touched the face, chest, arms, feet and toes. He then invited the others to come up to view the body. Finally the cloths were replaced over the body, the coffin lid was nailed down, and the coffin itself wrapped in silk and linen.

Abbot Samson's new shrine lasted until its destruction in 1539 at the Dissolution of the Monasteries under King Henry VIII. We can gain an impression of what it looked like from Jocelin's account and 15th century illustrations[31]. It was situated in the apse immediately behind the high altar of the church. Samson raised it on a stepped plinth, possibly of purple marble, so it could now be seen from the nave. It had an ornate stone base in early Gothic style. There is some evidence from Jocelin that the original base was hollow so that pilgrims could also crawl under the shrine and make their devotions close to the body of the saint.

The casing or lid of the shrine was shaped like a gabled building made of heavy, gilded silver panels studded with precious stones. It had a wooden cover suspended over it which could be raised or lowered at will. This cover proved its worth during a terrible fire in 1465, which destroyed the whole roof and the central tower and spire of the church. The cover was in its usual suspended position when it caught fire, but the rope burned through and the cover fell in flames, providentially covering the shrine and protecting its sacred contents.

Many offerings were added to the saint's resting place over the years. King Richard the Lionheart gave a banner captured from the King of Cyprus on a Crusade; his brother King John donated a large sapphire and a ruby set in gold; King Henry III gave a 'fine crown with four flowers on its rim worth £10 in all' to be attached to the shrine; two golden crosses, one worth 66s 8d, were donated by Henry de Lacy, Earl of Lincoln, one of which was decorated with a large ruby; some Dunwich fishermen hung up an anchor made of wax in gratitude for their safe delivery from a storm at sea; in 1457 Lady Ela Shardelowe bequeathed a gold brooch in the shape of a heart with angels, a ruby and four white enamel pendants. The humblest pilgrims no doubt offered a candle at the very least.

The area of the shrine was decorated with other cult objects, including a chest containing the venerable bones of Abbot Leofstan, Egelwin and Oswen.

Embroidered hangings hung close by, among them one depicting eleven scenes from the life of the saint.

St Edmund's shrine received many royal pilgrims. In a practice dating back to the days of Knut, kings would ritually send their crowns to the saint and then redeem them with an expensive gift. King Edward the Confessor was an especial devotee of the saint, and on reaching Bury he would dismount and respectfully walk the last mile on foot. After the death of Thomas à Beckett, Henry II came to pray and make his confession to Abbot Samson. Edward I is said to have visited the shrine thirteen times. In 1433 King Henry VI spent Christmas and the following Easter at the Abbey. He was later presented with a beautifully illustrated account in verse of the life of St Edmund, the 'Lives of SS Edmund and Fremund', written by John Lydgate[32].

Moche Vanitie and Supersticion

The Abbey in the early 16th century must have been a splendid sight. 'A man that saw the Abbay would say verily it were a Citie, so many gates there are in it, and some of brasse, so many Towres, and a most stately Church'; so wrote John Leland, the King's Antiquary, in 1538[33]. But times were changing. Two Royal Commissioners visited Bury two years earlier and reported on the state of the Abbey. "Amongst the relics we founde moche vanitie and supersticion, as the coles that S. Lawrence was tosted withal, the parings of St Edmund's naylles, S. Thomas of Canterbury penneknyff and his bootes, and divers skulls for the hedache… ". Interestingly, they made no mention of the saint's body among the relics.

There is some evidence that Edmund's relics may have been removed and taken to Toulouse in France. This story has been taken up in detail by recent Roman Catholic writers[34]. An inventory of sacred relics in the basilica of St Cernin at Toulouse was made in 1489, and recorded a body: 'Item... St Aymond, once the king of England'. It is now claimed that this entry referred to the relics of St Edmund. The presence of the relics in Toulouse is explained by theft: it is supposed that they were removed by the soldiers of Prince Louis of France during the Barons' Wars in 1217. However the only authority for a visit by his troops to Bury is a short passage in an anonymous French history of the Dukes of Normandy, which says he sent a detachment there in search of plunder[35].

In 1901 the skull became separated from the remainder of its bones when Pope Leo XIII authorised the transfer of the latter to England for installation in the new Westminster Cathedral. These relics were never transferred to the Cathedral because of a controversy about their authenticity, and have since remained at Arundel Castle in Sussex, in the care of the Dukes of Norfolk. The skull has remained in Toulouse, although three teeth from its upper jaw were transferred to Bury in 1966.

In 1539 Thomas Cromwell's Commissioners arrived at Bury to oversee the dissolution of the Abbey. They reported: "Pleaseth your Lordship to be advertised that we have been at Saynt Edmondsbury, where we found a riche shryne which was very comberous to deface. We have taken in the seyd monastery in golde and silver 5000 markes and above, besyds as well a riche crosse with emeralds, as also dyvers and sundry stones of great value".

How times had changed! In the 11th century Osgod Clapa had been driven mad for daring to stand with his axe next to the shrine. Cromwell's workmen set about stripping the lead from the roof of the church and demolishing its fabric with crowbars and gunpowder. 'Greater loss than this, so far as the works of man go, England never suffered', wrote William Camden[36]. No mention was made of the contents of the shrine. The body of St Edmund was of no concern to Cromwell's henchmen, nor was it any longer the business of the abbot and his band of 42 remaining monks as they faced a brave new world outside the Abbey walls.

6. LEGACY

Popular awareness of St Edmund dwindled after the dissolution of the monasteries, and devotion to the saints was forced underground or overseas as England became a Protestant country. It was left to overseas monasteries such as that of St Edmund's at Paris and later Douai to continue the Benedictine tradition at Bury. Vestiges of devotion also remained in ordinary English parish churches, albeit 'rebaptised' for Protestant use and often purged of their Mediaeval religious art.

There are over 60 churches and many chapels dedicated to St Edmund in England, and there are many examples of surviving church art featuring the saint, including carved roof bosses and bench ends, stained-glass, painted walls and panels. The typical emblems of the saint are a crowned male figure standing with one or more arrows; a crowned, severed head with attendant wolf; a crowned male figure tied to a tree, shot with arrows and beset by archers.

The 19th century saw a revival of interest in St Edmund centred on the village of Hoxne. The two chapels there had fallen out of use in the 16th century, and the Priory buildings had become partly incorporated into Abbey Farm[37]. However devotion to the saint was remembered by local people in the 18th century, who told stories about a Gold Bridge

associated with his death that was reputed to be perilous for newly married couples to cross. The 'Suffolk Garland' (1818) gave a version of the story in which St Edmund cursed a bridge under which he had been hiding: he had been betrayed to the Danes by a honeymooning couple who saw the gleam of his spurs reflected in the water. This story was given new impetus in 1878 when a new 'Goldbrook Bridge' was constructed in antiquarian style by a local landowner Sir Edward Kerrison.

Local tradition about St Edmund was also reflected in a story attached to an oak tree. In the early 14th century Robert Manning of Brunne had mentioned a tree at Hoxne, which suggests that the reputed tree of the martyrdom was among the experiences available to pilgrims. In 1848 an old oak near Abbey Farm is said to have collapsed, and on being sawn up an iron spike or arrow-head was found embedded in the wood. This may have encouraged people to assume that the two trees were identical. It is not clear how much of a real tradition there was surrounding this tree. A correspondent with local knowledge in the 'Gentleman's Magazine' for that year said it had always been known as Belmore's Oak, and denied hearing of any connection with St Edmund. A stone memorial now commemorates the spot.

Patron Saint of England

Until the early 11th century St Edmund had been venerated as a local, East Anglian saint. As we have seen, the story of the death of Svein had elevated him to new status as a supernatural protector of the English. However this status began to change from the 12th century onwards under the influence of the Crusades, as St George and his feast day became more widely venerated in England and he became the symbol of chivalry[38].

By the time of the Hundred Years' War, St Edmund had been eclipsed as England's patron saint, and today the flag of St George alone is fervently waved at English football matches. However, in 2007 a media-led campaign delivered a petition to the British government asking them to reinstate St Edmund as patron saint of England[39]. Although the government declined the request, Suffolk County Council officially adopted him as Patron Saint of Suffolk, and a special Suffolk flag featuring an emblem of the saint on the flag of St George has been designed.

The possibility of miracles is extremely attractive. It suggests divine providence may sometimes break through the order of nature and bring about unforeseen effects. 'Miracle' comes from Latin word *mirari*, to wonder at.

Tame wolves, non-decaying corpses, instances of sudden injury, healing or salvation: for Abbo and other devotees such wonder stories represented revelations of divine power 'over and above nature' and thus confirmed Edmund's sainthood. Can severed heads talk or paraplegics suddenly start leaping? In the world of stories they certainly can.

We may see Edmund's legacy as a body of mixed historical, legendary, mythical and skeletal material. It has been shaped and transmitted down the centuries by popular interest and by devoted belief and imagination. Like Sir Thomas Browne, we must rely on critical judgement to sort out fact from fable[40].

A martyred king; a miracle-working saint; a gilded shrine; a mighty abbey: Edmund's legacy is truly a casket of wonders.

ENDNOTES

[1] The 8th century 'Life of St Guthlac' includes evidence for Celtic-speaking people living in the Fenland c.700. Some East Anglians may have retained Celtic language until the 11th century (Morris 1995).

[2] Anglian, Saxon, Jutish, Frisian, Swabian and Swedish immigrant groups are thought to have made a contribution to the population of East Anglia in the centuries following the end of Roman rule. Estimates of their contribution vary between 10 and 30% (Oppenheimer 2006).

[3] The population of London in 800 is estimated to have been 4000 (Werner 1998).

[4] This impressive bank and ditch system is 7 miles (11.5km) long, stretching from high ground at Woodditton to fenland at Reach in Cambridgeshire. It may have been built to defend East Anglia from aggression by the kingdom of Mercia in the 7th and 8th centuries.

[5] The *Passio Sancti Eadmundi* by Abbo of Fleury was written in 985 when he was staying at Ramsey Abbey, Cambridgeshire, some 115 years after Edmund's death. Abbo was a monk and international scholar, abbot of the Benedictine monastery of Fleury sur Loire in France. See Hervey 1907 for text.

[6] Geoffrey of Wells was author of an imaginative *De Infantia Sancti Edmundi* (The Infancy of Saint Edmund). He is thought to have been based at Thetford Priory, c.1150.

[7] Botolph (Botwulf) was a seventh century monk who established a monastery at Icanho, probably Iken beside the River Alde in Suffolk. His remains were transferred to Bury Abbey in the early 11th century.

[8] This text (Bodley MS 240) was used by John Lydgate as the source for his 'Lives of SS Edmund and Fremund' (see Edwards 2004). For Siwara and Alkmund see Hervey 1907, p.XXIX.

[9] The Anglo-Saxon Chronicle is our most important source of historical information about Anglo-Saxon England. Nine manuscript copies have survived; the earliest is based on an original begun in Wessex in the late 9th century (Garmonsway 1954).

[10] This is a folktale motif. According to Irish myths, the god Balor of the Evil Eye had similar powers.

[11] Roger of Wendover (d.1236) was a monk at St Albans. He wrote a Latin chronicle covering the period from the Creation to 1235.

[12] Thomas of Elmham (d. c.1420), chronicler and monk at Canterbury. An European folktale motif features a bear who claims a human bride and then dies after the marriage is consummated.

[13] Saxo Grammaticus compiled his *Gesta Danorum* (History of the Danes) c.1200. It treated of the deeds of kings and heroes, drawn from ancient poems and chronicles. See Ellis Davidson 1996.

[14] The *Völsunga Saga* is a 13th century Icelandic saga relating the origin and decline of the Volsung clan. See <http://omacl.org/Volsunga/> (accessed July 2008).

[15] Hellesden Ley is a field name at Pitcher's Green on the 1840 Tithe Map for the parish of Bradfield St Clare (West 1982). Hervey (1907) makes a case for Hollesley and nearby Sutton as locations for the martyrdom and burial.

[16] Compare these stories with those of heavenly lights appearing at night over the relics of St Oswald of Northumbria (see Bede Book 3, Chapter 2).

[17] St Aelfheah (Alphege) was martyred by the Danes at Canterbury in 1012. The Anglo-Saxon Chronicle relates that he had refused to allow himself to be ransomed. He was pelted to the ground with the bones and heads of cattle then finished off with an axe.

[18] Greensted church at Chipping Ongar. This is the oldest wooden church in the world, and is built of plank-sawn timber, recently dated to the 11th century.

[19] These privileges included creation of The Liberty of St Edmund, which comprised the eight and a half hundreds (administrative districts) of West Suffolk, in which royal jurisdiction was delegated to the Abbey. It became the foundation of the Abbey's future wealth and influence (Warner 1996).

[20] Hermann was a monk at Bury c.1095. Samson was Abbot 1182-1212.

[21] Osgod or Osgoth, nicknamed Clapa (the Goggle-eyed) held the post of staller or master of the royal stables, and was a major landowner in East Anglia.

[22] Bury Abbey was a stupendous 505ft / 154m in length (compare Durham Cathedral 496 ft/ 143m; York Minster 485ft / 148m; Cologne Cathedral 474ft / 144.5m; Norwich Cathedral 460ft / 140m).

[23] Jurmin is probably a form of the name Eormen, the son of King Anna (Onna) of East Anglia, d.653 (Plunkett 2005).

[24] Herbert de Losinga was born near Argentan in Normandy. He was the first Bishop of Norwich, and founded Norwich Cathedral in 1096.

[25] King Aethelbert of East Anglia was beheaded on the orders of Offa of Mercia c.794, and canonized as St Aethelbryht. (Warner 1996).

[26] The chapel at Hoxne Priory was known as the Great Chapel. The new chapel was known as the New Worke, and stood on a hillside near Nuttery Vale, Hoxne (Carey Evans 1986).

[27] Compare the entries for Hoxne and Hellesdon in Ekwall (1960).

[28] Giraldus Cambrensis (c.1146-1223) was a Norman-Welsh churchman, author of the *Itinerarium Cambriae* ('Journey through Wales'), in which this story is told (Book 1, Chapter 2), written c.1194. Gerald says this story is contemporary.

[29] This banner is illustrated in Lydgate's 'Lives of SS. Edmund and Fremund' (Edwards 2004).

[30] Jocelin of Brakelond was a monk at Bury Abbey and chaplain to Abbot Samson. He wrote a chronicle *De Rebus Gestis Samsonis Abattis Monasterii Sancti Edmundi* which recounts events in the life of the monastery between 1173 and 1202 (Greenway & Sayers 1989).

[31] The shrine is depicted in John Lydgate's 'Lives of SS Edmund and Fremund', c.1434, however the pictures are the work of at least three artists and are not consistent with each other, so create uncertainties for interpretation (Edwards 2004).

[32] John Lydgate (c.1370-1449) was the pre-eminent English poet of the 15th century, and had long-established connections with Bury. St Fremund was a supposed nephew of Edmund who lived as a hermit; he is said to have led the English into battle after his uncle's death and 40,000 Danes were killed. See Edwards 2004.

[33] John Leland (c.1506-1552), King's Antiquary, employed by Henry VIII to search out and preserve ancient records and manuscripts in England. See Holland 1610.

[34] Mackinlay 1893; Houghton 1970.

[35] The theft of relics was common practice in the 13th century. The Crusaders plundered relics from Eastern Orthodox churches, and Roger of Wendover says it was behaviour typical of French soldiers. See Scarfe 1969.

[36] William Camden, antiquary and historian, author of *Britannia* (first edition published 1586); quoted in Mackinlay 1893, p.402.

[37] Carey Evans 1986.

[38] In the 14th century King Edward II adopted St George as patron of his new Order of the Garter.

[39] The petition was coordinated by BBC Radio Suffolk and the East Anglian Daily Times.

[40] Sir Thomas Browne (1605-1682), scientist and mystic, author of 'Pseudodoxia Epidemica' which wittily examined a range of 'popular errors' and commonly held beliefs.

REFERENCES AND FURTHER READING

Warm thanks are given to Hervey (1907) for assembling so many useful texts, particularly Abbo of Fleury, and to Mackinlay (1893) for his diligence in researching the Edmund corpus – he is truly the Saint's Biographer. Particular thanks must also go to Margaret Carey Evans, Norman Scarfe, Stanley West and Dorothy Whitelock for lighting the way with their scholarship.

Ashwin, T. & Davison, A. (eds): An Historical Atlas of Norfolk (Phillimore, Chichester; 2005)

Blunt, C.E.: The St Edmund Memorial Coinage (Proceedings of Suffolk Institute of Archaeology, XXXI; 1969)

Carey Evans, M.: The Contribution of Hoxne to the Cult of St Edmund, King and Martyr (Proceedings of Suffolk Institute of Archaeology & History, XXXVI; 1986)

Carr, R.D., Tester, A. & Murphy, P.: The Middle-Saxon Settlement at Staunch Meadow, Brandon (Antiquity, 235; 1988)

Crook, J. (1998): The architectural setting of the cult of St Edmund, in: Gransden (1998)

Dymond, D. & Martin, E. (eds): An Historical Atlas of Suffolk (Suffolk County Council; 1999)

Edwards, A. (ed): The Life of St Edmund King and Martyr: John Lydgate's illustrated verse life presented to Henry VI (The British Library; 2004)

Ekwall, E.: The Concise Oxford Dictionary of English Place-names (4th edtn, Oxford University Press; 1960)

Ellis Davidson, H. (ed): Saxo Grammaticus. The History of the Danes, Books I-IX (Boydell & Brewer, Woodbridge; 1996)

Garmonsway, G.N. (transl): The Anglo-Saxon Chronicle (Dent, London; 1954)

Gem, R. & Keen, L. (1981) Late Anglo-Saxon finds from the site of St Edmund's Abbey (Proceedings of Suffolk Institute of Archaeology, XXXV; 1998)

Gransden, A. (ed): Bury St Edmunds. Mediaeval Art, Architecture, Archaeology and Economy (British Academy; 1998)

Greenway, D. & Sayers, S. (transl): Jocelin of Brakelond: Chronicle of the Abbey of Bury St Edmunds (Oxford University Press; 1989)

Gurdon, Lady C.: County Folk-lore. Printed Extracts No.2. Suffolk (D. Nutt, London; 1893)

Hervey, Lord F.: Corolla Sancti Eadmundi: The Garland of Saint Edmund King and Martyr (John Murray, London; 1907)

Houghton, B.: Saint Edmund King and Martyr (Terence Dalton, Lavenham; 1970)

Holland, P. (transl): William Camden: Britain, or, a Chorographicall Description of the most flourishing Kingdomes, England, Scotland and Ireland (1610) (Online transcription at <http://www.visionofbritain.org.uk> (accessed June 2008))

James, M.R. (ed): On the Abbey of St Edmund at Bury (Cambridge Antiquarian Society; 1895)

Jones, G.: A History of the Vikings (Book Club Associates, London; 1973)

Mackinlay, J.B.: Saint Edmund King and Martyr (Art and Book Company, London; 1893)

Monsen, E. (ed): Heimskringla or the Lives of the Norse Kings (Heffer, Cambridge; 1932)

Morris, J.: The Age of Arthur (Orion Books Ltd, London; 1995)

Oppenheimer, S.: The Origins of the British: A genetic detective story (Constable, London; 2006)

Plunkett, S.J.: Suffolk in Anglo-Saxon Times (Tempus, Stroud; 2005)

Scarfe, N.: The Body of St Edmund – an Essay in Necrobiography (Proceedings of Suffolk Institute of Archaeology, XXXI; 1969)

Turner, N. & Jones, D. (eds): Selig Suffolk. A Catalogue of Religious Art (Ipswich Borough Council Museums and Galleries; undated)

Warner, P.: The Origins of Suffolk (Manchester University Press; 1996)

Werner, A. (ed): London Bodies (Museum of London; 1998).

West, S.E.: A new site for the martyrdom of St Edmund? (Proceedings of Suffolk Institute of Archaeology & History, XXXV; 1982)

Whitelock, D.: Fact and Fiction in the Legend of St Edmund (Proceedings of Suffolk Institute of Archaeology & History, XXXI; 1970)

Whitelock, D.: The Beginnings of English Society (2nd rev. edtn, Penguin, Harmondsworth; 1974)

Williamson, T.: The Origins of Norfolk (Manchester University Press; 1993)

ABOUT:

TIM HOLT WILSON gained a degree in Classical Studies and has developed specialist interests in East Anglian Archaeology and Natural History, particularly Quaternary Geology. He has worked for many years in heritage management and interpretation, including six years as a museum curator. He has authored a website on the history of Redgrave Park and is planning a book on the life and times of Thomas Paine.

BRIAN WHELAN was trained at The Royal Academy of Art in London. He is a London-Irish artist who moved his studio to East Anglia in search of medieval remnants of art he considered his heritage. His painting The Martyrdom of St. Edmund is permanently installed in the St. Edmundsbury Cathedral. Other works of his are installed in The Legion of St. Gabriel's Language School in Czestochowa Poland and St Benedict's Abbey in west London; and can be found in private collections throughout the world. www.brianwhelan.co.uk